Level Three

Compiled and arranged by Wesley Schaum
CD orchestrations by Jeff Schaum

FOREWORD

This series offers students an appealing variety of styles in a single album. A brief paragraph of background information is provided for many pieces. Folk music includes spirituals. Jazz styles include boogie, blues, ragtime, swing and rock.

All books include a CD with orchestrated accompaniments. Each piece has two CD tracks: 1) Performance tempo 2) Practice tempo.

The intent of the CD is to provide an incentive for practice by demonstrating how the finished piece will sound. The slower practice tempo assists the student in maintaining a steady beat, using the correct rhythm and gaining valuable ensemble experience while making practice more fun.

A performance /practice CD is enclosed in an envelope attached to the back inside cover.

INDEX

Schaum Publications, Inc.
10235 N. Port Washington Rd. • Mequon, WI 53092
www.schaumpiano.net

03-63
KT-1

You're a Grand Old Flag

Con vivo ♩ = 108-120

Words and music by George M. Cohan

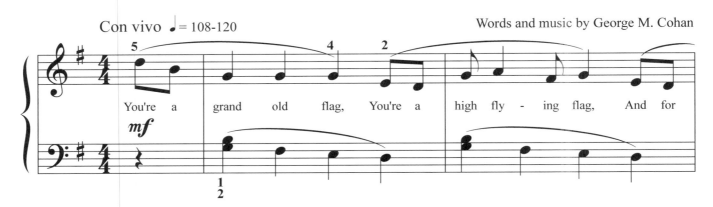

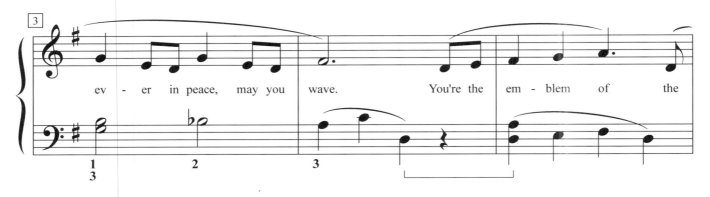

CD Track 1: Performance tempo
CD Track 2: Practice tempo (played twice)
(Each track includes two-measure introduction)

George Michael Cohan was born in Providence, Rhode Island in 1878. His parents were traveling musicians who performed in vaudeville shows in local theaters. Vaudeville was a variety show which included musical acts, acrobats, jugglers, magicians, comedians and trained animals. By the time he was nine years old, George was singing and dancing as part of his parents' act. By age 11 he was writing special material and by age 13 he was writing songs and lyrics for the family act.

"You're a Grand Old Flag" is from a play he wrote in 1906 titled, *Mary's a Grand Old Name.* During the performance he marched up and down the stage carrying the American flag while singing this song.

During his lifetime George M. Cohan wrote 40 plays, made over 1000 appearances as an actor on stage and in film and wrote more than 500 songs. "I'm a Yankee Doodle Dandy" and "Give My Regards To Broadway" are among his best known songs.

Easy Winners

Scott Joplin

Moderato ♩ = 108-120

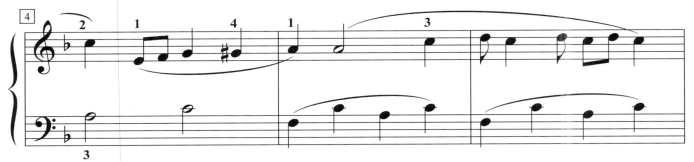

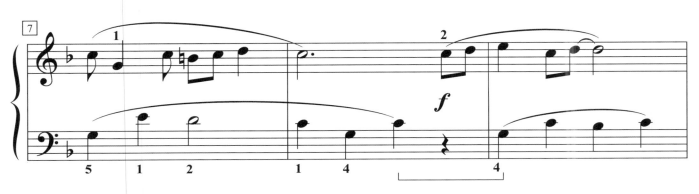

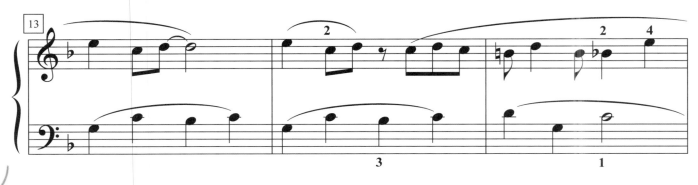

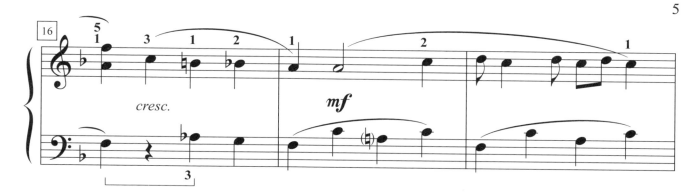

"Easy Winners" is a phrase used by gamblers at a horse racing track. It describes horses that are considered almost certain to win the race in which they compete.

Scott Joplin was an African-American composer famous for his ragtime music written for piano. He lived from 1868 to 1917. "Easy Winners" was written in 1901.

This music, along with other ragtime pieces by Scott Joplin, was part of the soundtrack for an Academy Award winning 1974 movie titled "The Sting." The movie was about a small group of men who create an elaborate horse racing scheme to cheat wealthy gamblers out of their money. The movie is available on video cassette or DVD.

CD Track 3:   Performance tempo
CD Track 4:   Practice tempo (played twice)

Chip Dip

Con moto ♩ = 112-126 *(swing 8ths)*

Wesley Schaum

CD Track 5: **Performance tempo**
CD Track 6: **Practice tempo (played twice)**

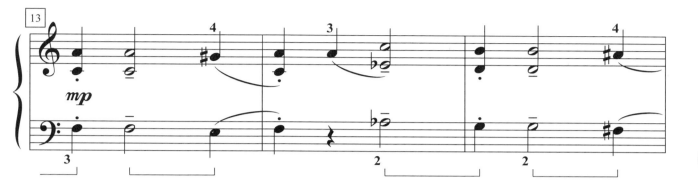

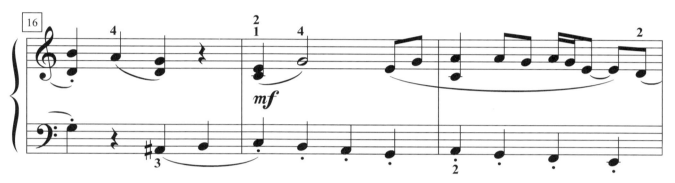

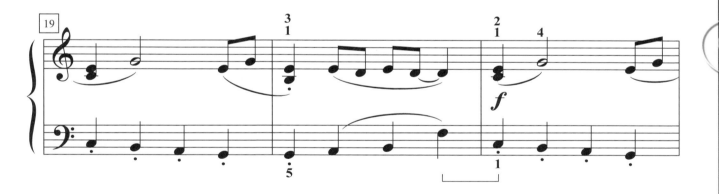

La Cucaracha

Giocoso ♩ = 104-116

Mexican Folk Song

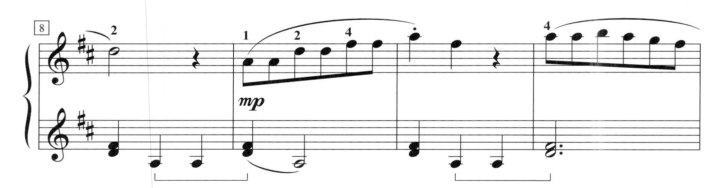

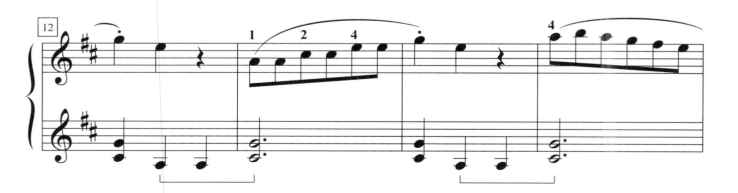

 CD Track 7: **Performance tempo**
CD Track 8: **Practice tempo (played twice)**

This folk song is said to have originated in the Mexican state of Chihuahua (chee-WAH-wah) in the early 1900's during a social revolt. This song was probably sung by Mexican revolutionary soldiers during military maneuvers and for evening campfire entertainment. (Chihuahua is also the name of a small dog first bred in Mexico.)

The song has a great variety of verses, most of them humorous and many referring to Mexican revolutionary leaders or groups. Singers often made up new verses as they went along. Some verses refer to different regions in Mexico. In Spanish, "La Cucaracha" means "the cockroach."

Anchors Aweigh

Revised words by John W. Schaum

Charles A. Zimmerman

"Anchors Aweigh" means that a ship lifts its anchor and starts moving. This is the official song of the United States Navy.

Charles A. Zimmerman was a former Music Director of the U.S. Naval Academy in Annapolis, Maryland. The Academy is a special military college established in 1845. Studies include mathematics, science and engineering as well as navigation and naval weaponry. Men and women who graduate become officers in the Navy or Marine Corps. Many graduates spend their entire career in the navy.

CD Track 9: Performance tempo
CD Track 10: Practice tempo (played twice)

He's Got the Whole World In His Hands

Andante ♩ = 88-100 *(swing 8ths)*

African-American Spiritual

Spirituals are religious folk songs which originated with African Americans in the southern United States in the late 1700's and early 1800's. The words for many spirituals are based on stories and characters from the Bible and were sung at religious meetings. Other spirituals were sung while people worked.

In those days, musical instruments were rare, so spirituals were usually unaccompanied. Rhythm was sometimes provided by clapping hands. The verses often have sections sung by a soloist alternating with sections sung by a group.

CD Track 11: Performance tempo
CD Track 12: Practice tempo (played twice)

14

Lullaby

Lento ♩ = 72-80

Johannes Brahms, Op. 49, No. 4

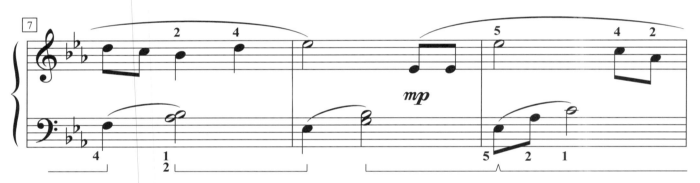

 CD Track 13: Performance tempo
CD Track 14: Practice tempo (played twice)

Toreador March
(from "Carmen")

George Bizet

Marziale ♩ = 92-104

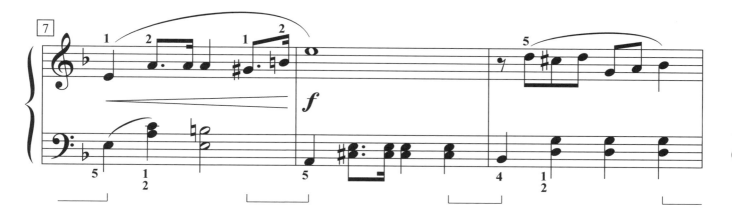

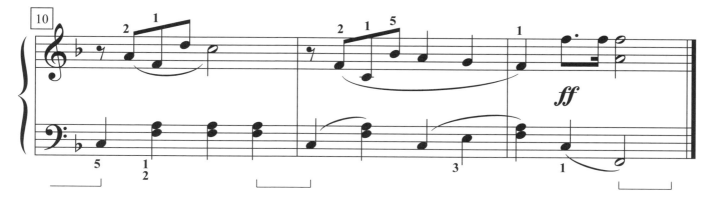

CD Track 15: Performance tempo
CD Track 16: Practice tempo (played twice)

Oh! Susanna

Con vivo ♩ = 138-160

Stephen Foster

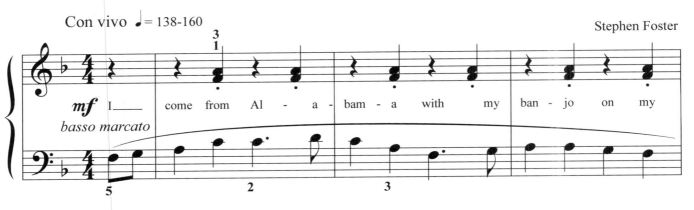

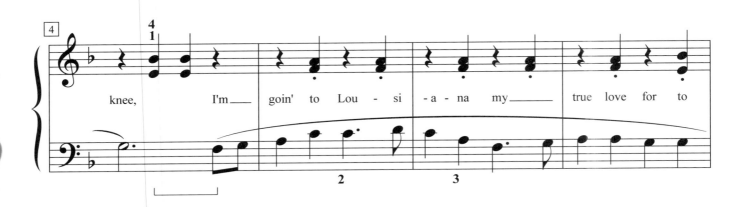

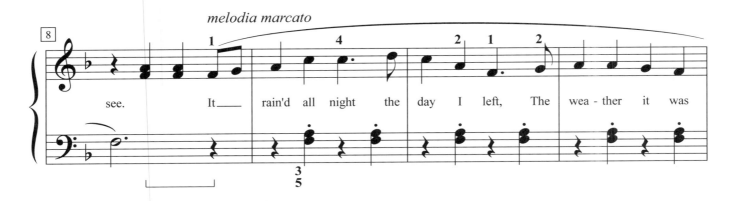

 CD Track 17: Performance tempo
CD Track 18: Practice tempo (played twice)

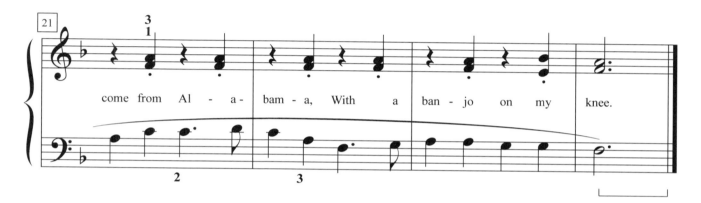

Stephen Foster (1826-1864) was born in a small town near Pittsburgh, Pennsylvania. He was almost entirely self-trained as a composer.

"Oh! Susanna" was first performed in 1847 and established his reputation as a songwriter. Of the nearly 200 songs he wrote, about a dozen remain well known.

Long after this death, Foster was honored by being the first American musician elected to the Hall of Fame at New York University. His manuscripts and papers are preserved at Foster Hall at the University of Pittsburgh. His song, "Old Folks At Home" is the official state song of Florida. Foster's "My Old Kentucky Home" is Kentucky's official state song.

London Bridge Swing

Vivace ♩ = 126-144 *(swing 8ths)*

Wesley Schaum

mf Lon - don bridge is | fall - ing down, | fall - ing down, | fall - ing down.

Lon - don bridge is | fall - ing down, | My fair | la - dy.

Variation 1

Variation 2

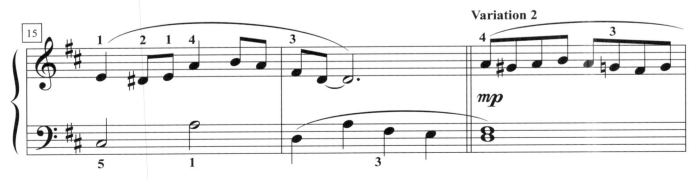

CD Track 19: Performance tempo
CD Track 20: Practice tempo (played twice)

Variation 3

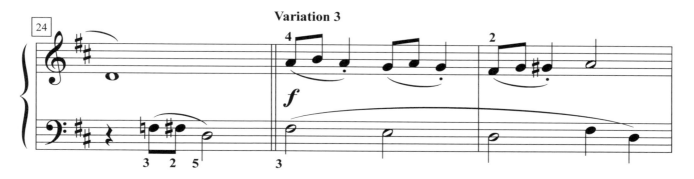

Star-Spangled Banner

Francis Scott Key

Maestoso ♩ = 92-100

John Stafford Smith

O say can you see by the dawn's ear - ly light, What so

proud - ly we hailed at the twi - light's last gleam - ing? Whose broad

stripes and bright stars through the per - il - ous fight. O'er the

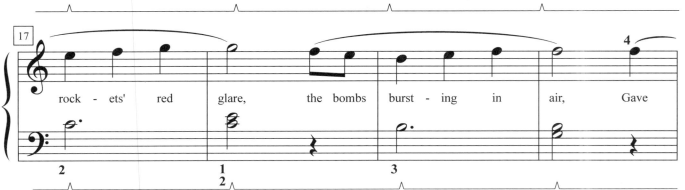

ram - parts we watched, were so gal - lant - ly stream - ing! And the

rock - ets' red glare, the bombs burst - ing in air, Gave

The words for the "Star-Spangled Banner" were written as a poem by Francis Scott Key during the War of 1812. In this poem, the word "banner" refers to a flag and "star-spangled" means sprinkled with stars. Key witnessed a British bombardment of Fort McHenry in Baltimore, Maryland. When the smoke cleared after many hours of bombing, and Key was able to see the huge American flag still waving, he knew that the fort had survived the bombing.

The next morning, the four verses of his poem were printed and distributed throughout Baltimore. Soon after, the words were sung to the tune of "To Anacreon in Heaven." This melody was familiar at the time as a military march and a political campaign song. Many years later, in 1931, the U.S. Congress made the "Star-Spangled Banner" the official national anthem of the United States.

CD Track 21: Performance tempo
CD Track 22: Practice tempo (played twice)

Spring Song

Felix Mendelssohn, Op. 62, No. 6

CD Track 23: Performance tempo
CD Track 24: Practice tempo (played twice)

March

(from "Nutcracker")

Moderato ♩ = 100-108

Peter I. Tchaikowsky

23

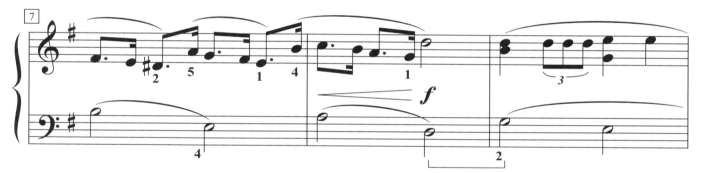

 CD Track 25: Performance tempo
CD Track 26: Practice tempo (played twice)

Successful Schaum Sheet Music

* = Big Notes   • = Original Form   ✓ = Chord Symbols

LEVEL TWO